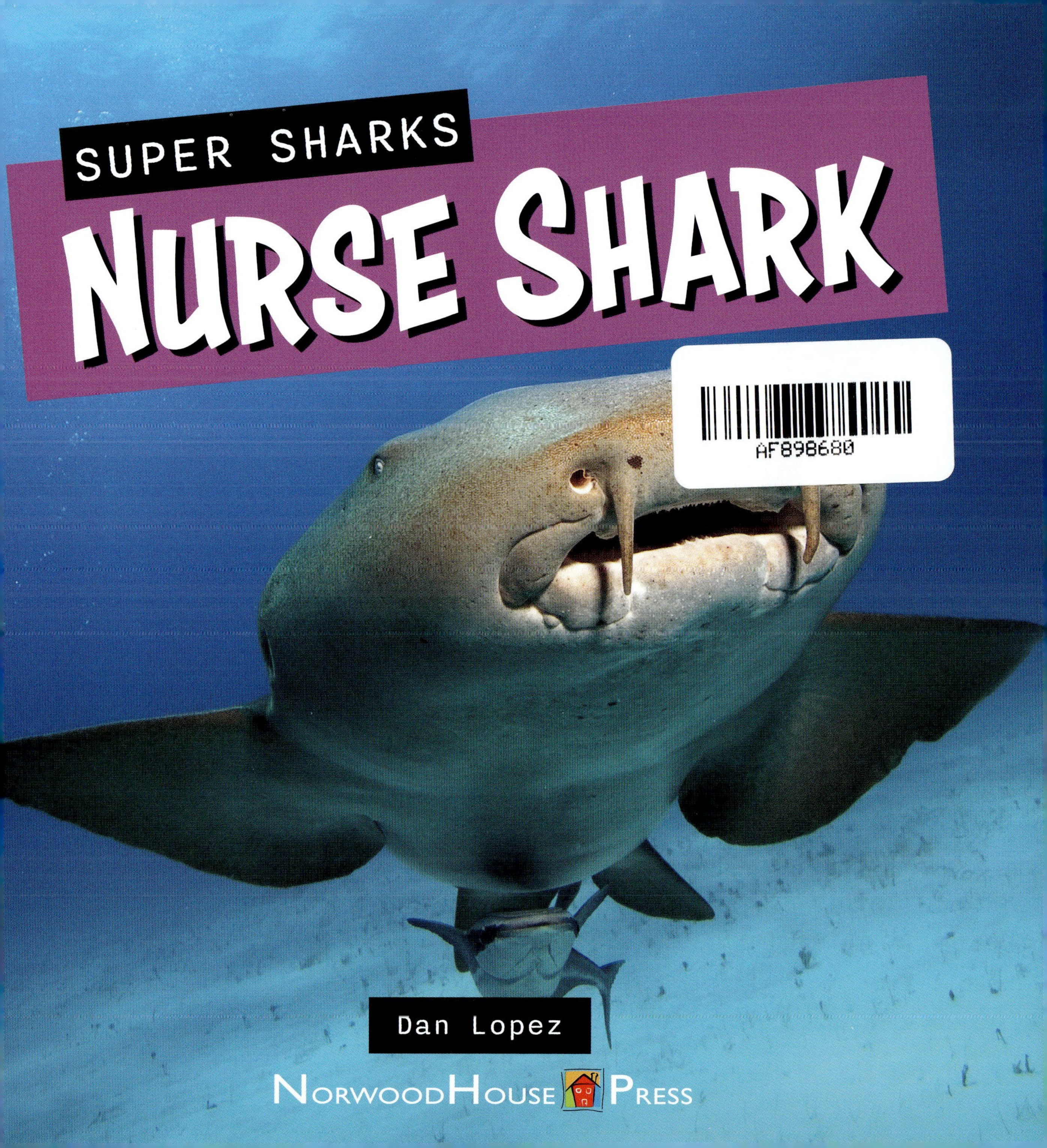

SUPER SHARKS

NURSE SHARK

Dan Lopez

NorwoodHouse Press

Cataloging-in-Publication Data

Names: Lopez, Dan.
Title: Nurse shark / Dan Lopez.
Description: Buffalo, NY : Norwood House Press, 2027. | Series: Super sharks | Includes glossary and index.
Identifiers: ISBN 9781978581401 (pbk.) | ISBN 9781978581418 (library bound) | ISBN 9781978581425 (ebook)
Subjects: LCSH: Nurse shark--Juvenile literature.
Classification: LCC QL638.95.G55 L67 2027 | DDC 597.33--dc23

Published in 2027 by
Norwood House Press
2544 Clinton Street
Buffalo, NY 14224

Designer: Rhea Magaro
Editor: Tricia Hoffman

Photo credits: Cover, p. 1 frantisekhojdysz/Shutterstock.com; p. 4 Damsea/Shutterstock.com; p. 5 MartinRejzek/Shutterstock.com; p. 6 Beat J Korner/Shutterstock.com; pp. 8, 21 Wonderful Nature/Shutterstock.com; p. 9 Daniel Lamborn/Shutterstock.com; p. 10 Maydel/Shutterstock.com; p. 12 Tica-memories/Shutterstock.com; p. 13 Somphob Boonlaim/Shutterstock.com; p. 14 Daryl Duda/Shutterstock.com; p. 15 Pete Niesen/Shutterstock.com; p. 17 Izen Kai/Shutterstock.com; p. 18 Martin Prochazkacz/Shutterstock.com;

Printed in the United States of America

CPSIA compliance information: Batch #CSNHP27: For further information contact Norwood House Press at 1-800-237-9932.

TABLE OF CONTENTS

What Is Special about Nurse Sharks?

Nurse sharks are gentle giants. These big fish swim slowly over the ocean floor. They do not harm people unless they are bothered.

Their name may come from the sucking motion they make as they eat. It looks like a baby nursing.

What Do Nurse Sharks Look Like?

Nurse sharks can be 14 feet (four meters) long. They can weigh 300 pounds (136 kilograms).

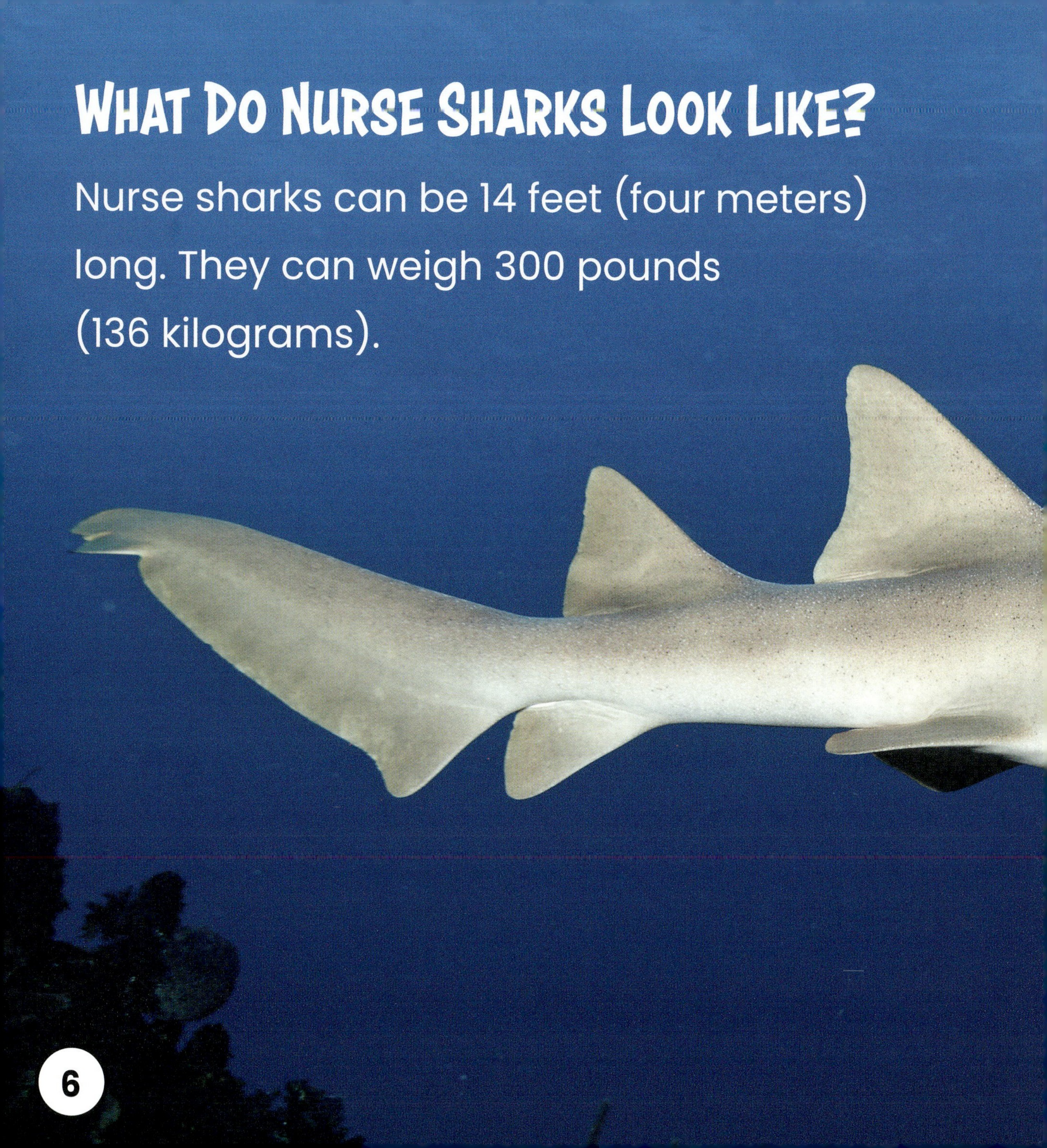

Their skin is gray-brown. It feels like sandpaper. A tail fin, **pectoral fins**, and **dorsal fins** help a nurse shark swim.

Unlike most sharks, nurse sharks don't have to swim in order to breathe. They can lie in one place and pump water over their **gills**.

Two soft **appendages** hang near the mouth. These are barbels. They are like a cat's whiskers. They help the shark sense food on the sandy ocean floor.

WHERE DO NURSE SHARKS LIVE?

These sharks swim in the Atlantic and Pacific Oceans. They are found in warm waters near the **coasts** of Africa, Central America, South America, and the United States.

At night, nurse sharks hunt. During the day, groups rest in caves and other protected places.

How Do Nurse Sharks Hunt?

Nurse sharks are bottom feeders. They swim along the seafloor and near **coral reefs**. Their barbels help them find food.

They are not picky. They eat lobsters, crabs, shrimp, fish, and just about anything else they find.

A nurse shark's mouth creates powerful **suction**. Food gets sucked in whole. The force is strong enough to rip a **mollusk** out of its shell.

About 75 small teeth grow in rows. They are not for biting. They are **serrated** to help the nurse shark grasp its prey. They are strong enough to crunch **crustacean** shells.

How Do Nurse Sharks Reproduce?

Eggs hatch inside the female's body. She gives birth to live babies, or pups.

New pups are one foot (30 centimeters) long. They will keep growing for about 20 years.

Glossary

appendages (uh-PEN-di-jiz): body parts attached to larger body parts; limbs

coasts (kohsts): areas of land near the sea

coral reefs (KOR-uhl reefs): large underwater structures that are made from the skeletons of tiny sea creatures and that provide habitat for many ocean animals

crustaceans (kruh-STAY-shuhns): sea creatures with hard outer skeletons, such as crabs, lobsters, and shrimp

dorsal fins (DOR-sl fins): flat, thin body parts that stick up from the back of a shark or other marine animal

gills (gilz): breathing organs near a fish's mouth that extract oxygen from water

mollusk (MAH-luhsk): an ocean animal with a soft body inside a hard shell, such as a snail or oyster

pectoral fins (PEK-tuh-ruhl finz): fins on both sides of an aquatic animal that act like arms to guide the animal through water

serrated (SER-ay-ted): notched like the blade of a saw

suction (SUHK-shuhn): the act of drawing air out of a space to make a vacuum that sucks things in

THINKING QUESTIONS

1. What does it mean to be a bottom feeder?
2. What are barbels?
3. Why doesn't a nurse shark have to swim in order to breathe?
4. How does a nurse shark use its teeth?
5. What do nurse sharks eat?

Index

About the Author

Dan Lopez lives far from the ocean in Indianapolis, Indiana, with his wife and three kids. He is fascinated by all of Earth's animals, including sharks! He admires their sleekness and speed and thinks more people should appreciate them.